A DK PUBLISHING BOOK

Project Editor Caroline Bingham
Art Editor Mike Buckley
Extra design help Anna Benckert,
Ivan Finnegan, Karen Lieberman

US Editor Camela Decaire
Deputy Managing Editor Mary Ling
Senior Art Editor Jane Horne

Production David Hyde
Picture research Ingrid Nilsson

**Photography, at risk to life
and limb, by** Frank Greenaway
and Kim Taylor

First American Edition 1996
2 4 6 8 10 9 7 5 3 1

Published in the United States by
DK Publishing, Inc., 95 Madison Avenue,
New York, New York 10016

Copyright © 1996 Dorling Kindersley Limited, London

Published in Great Britain by Dorling Kindersley
Limited.

Distributed by Houghton Mifflin Company, Boston.

A CIP catalog record for this book
is available from the Library of Congress.

ISBN: 0-7894-1118-0

Color reproduction by Colourscan
Printed in Italy by L.E.G.O.

The publisher would like to thank the following for
their kind permission to reproduce their photographs:
t top, b bottom, l left, r right, c centre.
Bruce Coleman/Dr. Frieder Sauer (Buzz Time: br)/Jan
Taylor (Dig In!: bl)/Kim Taylor (One to Avoid!: tl,
br/Buzz Time: tl, cb); NHPA/Anthony Bannister (this
page: Horsefly/Cut and Stab: tl)/Stephen Dalton (Cut
and Stab: bl)/Rod Planck (Cut and Stab: tr); Oxford
Scientific Films/London Scientific Films (Dig In!:
br)/Harold Taylor (Dig In!: three sheep ticks, center);
Premaphotos/R.A. Preston-Mafham (Buzz Time: bl,
Cut and Stab: cl); Jerry Young (Hairy Horrors: tl).

Hairy Horrors

The Tail End

Cut and Stab

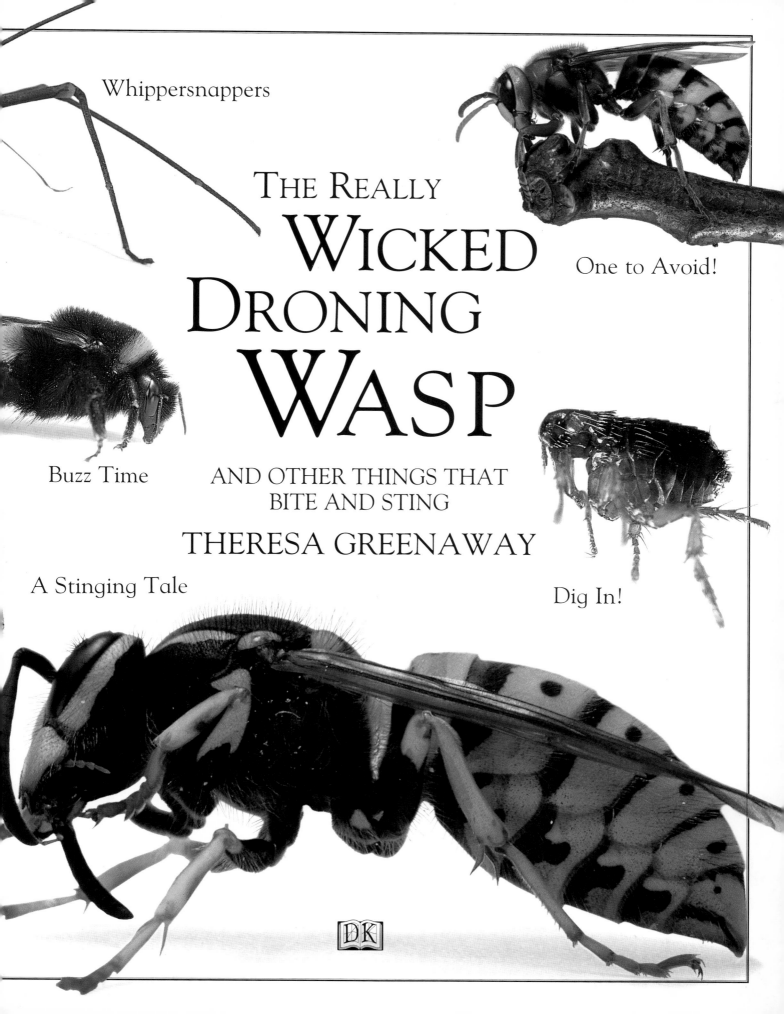

Whippersnappers

THE REALLY
WICKED
DRONING
WASP

One to Avoid!

Buzz Time

AND OTHER THINGS THAT
BITE AND STING

THERESA GREENAWAY

A Stinging Tale

Dig In!

DK

A STINGING TALE

Wasps are stinging insects that can be really annoying, especially in hot weather at the end of summer. But wasps are not all bad. Every day, wasps catch insects, including many that are pests, to feed to their young, or larvae.

Many wasps are social insects, living in nests with up to 2,000 others. The nests are made from chewed-up wood.

Tropical wasp

A nest contains female workers, drones (or male wasps), and a queen. Workers have stingers to use in self-defense, and can paralyze or kill their prey.

A jewel wasp's body-casing gleams in sunlight.

Jewel wasp

German wasp, queen

Ichneuman wasps lay their eggs inside other insects. The larvae feed on their host when they hatch.

Ichneuman wasp

A jewel wasp seizes prey in its fearsome jaws and stings deep into the victim's nerve center to paralyze it.

Jewel wasp

A female jewel wasp will drag her catch into a burrow, then lay an egg in it, like the Ichneuman wasp.

Unlike bees, wasps have straight stingers, and can sting again and again.

Only a queen wasp lays eggs. After setting up a nest, she feeds her first batch of larvae. As adults, they will take over the task of rearing young.

ONE TO AVOID!

Its size and the noise of its wings will strike terror into the heart of anyone who has a close encounter with a humming hornet, a large wasp. But don't worry; hornets usually live and hunt in woodlands, not in houses.

Hornet in flight

A hornet is the biggest stinging insect in the world.

Hornet

It hides its stinger in its tail.

Hornets search for insect prey using large compound eyes and sensitive antennae. Victims are taken to their nest, where they are chewed up, then fed to the hornet young, or grubs.

A hornet isn't afraid of wasps or bees. It can cut them in half with one swipe of its powerful, scissorlike jaws.

Hornet resting on an acorn

Because it's so large, a hornet's sting hurts a lot. Fortunately, hornets only sting humans if they feel threatened.

Not all hornets have the ability to sting. This drone, or male, looks fierce, but doesn't have a stinger.

Hornet workers can grow up to 1.25 in (33 mm) in length!

Male hornet

BUZZ TIME

Bees are useful. They pollinate flowers and many provide honey. But be careful! Bees can sting, and that's a powerful weapon.

Honeybee worker

Female bee

As a bee stings, a special mix of chemicals is pumped from a venom sac into the wound.

Honeybees live in enormous colonies of up to 50,000 bees.

Not all bees live in colonies. Some are solitary, with each female bee making her own small nest.

A bumble-bee's wings beat about 200 times per second!

It looks too heavy to fly, but it zips up to 10 mph.

Bees collect nectar from flowers to feed to their larva.

Carder-bee

Honeybee in flight

Honeybees have barbed stings. Once a sting is out, the bee cannot pull it back. When the bee flies away from its victim, part of its insides also get pulled out. The bee dies.

Stinging you means certain death for the bee.

Honeybee stinging

As honeybees fly along, their two pairs of wings make a distinctive buzz.

DIG IN!

All sorts of awful parasites live on the outside of animals, even on us. They are looking for blood to suck, and they have ways of making sure they stay put on their host.

Sheep tick

Flea

A flea's body is almost flat from side to side, so it can race through a host's fur.

For a sheep tick to get a meal, it must climb up a grass stem and hope for a passing animal to grab on to.

Sheep tick

Ticks are related to spiders. Adults have eight legs.

Kangaroo tick

A tick anchors itself to its host's skin with a toothed stabber called a hypostome.

It takes a few days for a tick to completely fill up with blood. It becomes so swollen it starts to look like a bean.

A young deer ked has wings and can fly to find a host. Once found, it burrows into the host's fur and sheds its wings.

A ked clings to a deer's fur with large hooks on its feet. Once it gets hold, it's very hard to shake off.

Deer ked

Sheep tick

Unlike a tick, a deer ked has six legs. This makes it a true insect.

Ticks may wait up to a year for a suitable host to pass by.

An adult female sheep tick lays as many as 18,000 eggs at once to allow for all the ticks that die because they can't find a host.

Sheep tick

HAIRY HORRORS

How can a juicy caterpillar avoid ending up as some other animal's dinner? Surprisingly, hairs do the trick, from hairs that snap off to hairs that inject poisonous fluids.

Tropical tiger moth caterpillar after molt

A tropical lappet moth caterpillar

This caterpillar is so well covered that a bird trying to peck it up just gets a beakful of hair.

A tropical tiger moth caterpillar

A tropical tiger moth caterpillar is truly nasty. Just brushing its hairs causes skin sores and an incurable arthritis in nearby joints.

When the bright yellow caterpillar molts, its next hairy jacket is gray.

Colonial
caterpillars
stay in groups
and can
produce toxins
if touched.

Colonial
caterpillars

When danger approaches, colonial caterpillars fling back their heads and thrash around wildly. Predators are tricked into thinking the group is one large animal.

A tropical
emperor moth
caterpillar

This alarming
caterpillar has long, sticky hairs,
making it really unpleasant for a
predator to eat. No one tries twice!

WHIPPERSNAPPERS

False whip scorpions are strange creatures. They hunt at night and hide in the day and so are rarely seen, even in the tropics where most of them live.

Even the largest of these beasts can fold up its long legs and vanish into a surprisingly narrow crack.

Sharp spines on the palps crush prey. The mangled

Spiny front grabbers called palps seize and crush up live prey. Then bits of food are passed to the jaws.

With their eight spindly legs, they are alarming to look at, but they're not poisonous.

Long front legs help the scorpion feel its way.

Six of a false whip scorpion's eight legs are used for running – very fast. The two incredibly long and thin legs at the front are used just like antennae.

From tip to tip the legs reach 6 in.

The leggy creatures climb easily over logs and rocks to hunt for insect prey.

whip scorpion's strong jaws.

chewed up in the false

victim is then

Prowling by night, these fierce predators will rush at and attack anything with their fearsome palps. They'd even give you a sharp bite if you got too close!

THE TAIL END

A large, apparently deadly scorpion frequently stars in scary films, but in fact, it's the small kinds that are the most dangerous – and only about 50 of the 1,200 species of scorpions are even likely to be dangerous to people.

Imperial scorpion

A scorpion's two eyes may look beady and sharp, but its sight is poor. It can only tell the difference between light and dark.

Pincers are used to hold down and rip apart a juicy grasshopper or tasty centipede meal.

Scorpions have eight legs to run with and a huge pair of pincers. The use these pincers like hands, gripping prey.

The venom of one African scorpion can kill a person within seven hours. The venom is carried in the tip of the tail.

Desert scorpion

A scorpion can survive without water for three months, and without food for twelve months!

Scorpion with babies

A scorpion gives birth to lots of tiny scorpions. They climb on their mother's back for two weeks, until they are stronger.

CUT AND STAB

Only female horseflies are bloodthirsty pirates. They need the nutrients in blood to be able to produce their eggs. Male horseflies prefer to spend their days buzzing lazily around, sipping nectar from flowers.

Horsefly cleaning its proboscis

To get blood, a female horsefly stabs into her victim's skin with a sharp, stout tube called a proboscis.

Horsefly

A horsefly leaves victims with large painful swellings.

Horsefly

However horrible its habits, a horsefly does clean up after a meal. It wipes its proboscis.

Blood stays runny and can be sucked up easily thanks to special chemicals in a horsefly's saliva.

Horsefly

A horsefly stabs and jabs at its victim – it can get through even the toughest hide. Then it begins to suck up the free-flowing blood.

A horsefly's large, jabbing mouthparts look very fierce.

Horseflies like to fly on warm, sunny days, when the smell of sweating animals helps them locate food sources. Their large, iridescent compound eyes are quick to pick up movement, too.

Horsefly

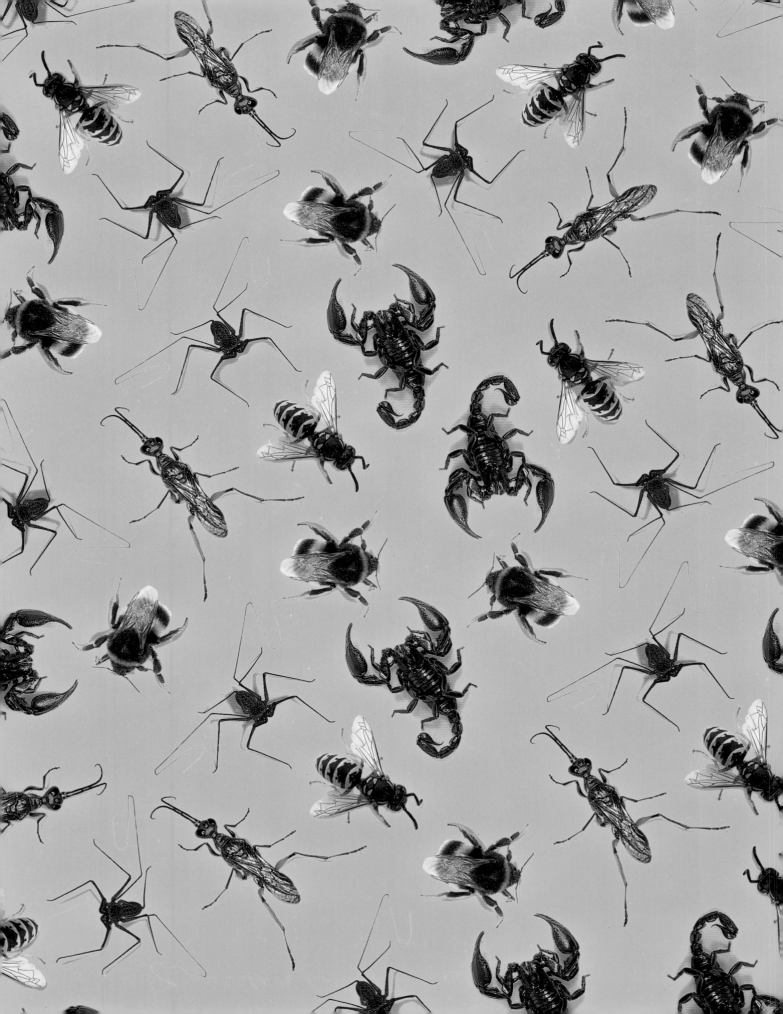